20 best
birthday cake
recipes for tots

Houghton Mifflin Harcourt
Boston • New York • 2013

Copyright © 2013 by General Mills, Minneapolis, Minnesota. All rights reserved.

For information about permission to reproduce selections from this book, write to Permissions, Houghton Mifflin Harcourt Publishing Company, 215 Park Avenue South, New York, New York 10003.

www.hmhco.com

Cover photo: First Birthday Lion Cake (page 9)

General Mills

Food Content and Relationship Marketing Director: Geoff Johnson
Food Content Marketing Manager: Susan Klobuchar
Senior Editor: Grace Wells
Kitchen Manager: Ann Stuart
Recipe Development and Testing: Betty Crocker Kitchens
Photography: General Mills Photography Studios and Image Library

Houghton Mifflin Harcourt

Publisher: Natalie Chapman
Editorial Director: Cindy Kitchel
Executive Editor: Anne Ficklen
Associate Editor: Heather Dabah
Managing Editor: Rebecca Springer
Production Editor: Kristi Hart
Cover Design: Chrissy Kurpeski
Book Design: Tai Blanche

ISBN 978-0-544-31466-5
Printed in the United States of America

The Betty Crocker Kitchens seal guarantees success in your kitchen. Every recipe has been tested in America's Most Trusted Kitchens™ to meet our high standards of reliability, easy preparation and great taste.

FIND MORE GREAT IDEAS AT
BettyCrocker.com

Dear Friends,

This new collection of colorful mini books has been put together with you in mind because we know that you love great recipes and enjoy cooking and baking but have a busy lifestyle. So every little book in the series contains just 20 recipes for you to treasure and enjoy. Plus, each book is a single subject designed in a bite-size format just for you—it's easy to use and is filled with favorite recipes from the Betty Crocker Kitchens!

All of the books are conveniently divided into short chapters so you can quickly find what you're looking for, and the beautiful photos throughout are sure to entice you into making the delicious recipes. In the series, you'll discover a fabulous array of recipes to spark your interest—from cookies, cupcakes and birthday cakes to party ideas for a variety of occasions. There's grilled foods, potluck favorites and even gluten-free recipes too.

You'll love the variety in these mini books—so pick one or choose them all for your cooking pleasure.

Enjoy and happy cooking!

Sincerely,

Betty Crocker

contents

Fun First Birthdays
First Birthday Smash Cake · 6
Cheerios First Birthday Cake · 7
Rubber Ducky Cake · 8
First Birthday Lion Cake · 9
Balloon Fun Cake · 10
Building Blocks Cakes · 11

Favorite Animals
Inchworm Cake · 12
Dinosaur Cake · 14
Easy Bunny Cakes · 16
Pull-Apart Turtle Cupcakes · 17
Pony Cake · 18
Panda Bear Cake · 20
Barn Cake with Farm Animal Cupcakes · 22

Theme Parties
Little Car Cakes · 24
Beary Fun Cupcake Cones · 25
Fire Engine Cake · 26
Party-Time Purse Cake · 28
Mermaid Cake · 30
Fairy Tale Princess Cake · 32
Castle Cake · 34

Metric Conversion Guide · 36
Recipe Testing and Calculating Nutrition Information · 37

Fun First Birthdays

First Birthday Smash Cake

Prep Time: 40 Minutes • **Start to Finish:** 1 Hour 15 Minutes • Makes 24 servings

- 1 box Betty Crocker® Super Moist® yellow cake mix
- 1 cup mashed very ripe bananas (2 medium)
- ½ cup vegetable oil
- ¼ cup water
- 3 eggs
- 1 package (8 oz) cream cheese, softened
- 1 container (6 oz) Yoplait®* Original 99% Fat Free French vanilla yogurt
- Golden yellow gel or paste food color
- ½ cup Cheerios® cereal

What fun to have a delicious cake that your child can smash!

1 Heat oven to 350°F (325°F for dark or nonstick pans). Grease with shortening or cooking spray bottom only of 1 (6-inch) round cake pan, and place paper baking cup in each of 16 regular-size muffin cups.

2 In large bowl, beat cake mix, bananas, oil, water and eggs with electric mixer on low speed 30 seconds. Beat on medium speed 2 minutes, scraping bowl occasionally until smooth. Place 1¾ cups batter in 6-inch round pan. Divide remaining batter evenly among 16 lined muffin cups. Bake round cake 35 to 40 minutes and cupcakes 18 to 23 minutes or until toothpick inserted in cake comes out clean. Cool 10 minutes; remove from pans to cooling racks. Cool completely, about 30 minutes.

3 In small bowl, beat cream cheese and yogurt on medium speed with electric mixer until creamy and smooth. Stir in food color until mixture is desired color.

4 Slice 6-inch round cake horizontally to remove rounded top. Place cake cut side down on plate. Frost top and side with cream cheese frosting. Place 2 rows of cereal around the bottom edge of side of cake. Place 1 row of cereal around top edge of cake. In top center of cake, arrange cereal to form the number "1."

5 Use remaining frosting to frost cupcakes. Top with cereal to decorate, if desired. Store cake and cupcakes in refrigerator.

1 Serving: Calories 170; Total Fat 9g (Saturated Fat 3g, Trans Fat 0g); Cholesterol 35mg; Sodium 190mg; Total Carbohydrate 20g (Dietary Fiber 0g); Protein 2g **Exchanges:** ½ Starch, 1 Other Carbohydrate, 1½ Fat **Carbohydrate Choices:** 1

Tip Are you short on time? Substitute Betty Crocker Whipped fluffy white frosting for the homemade frosting. Add the food color to make the desired color.

* Yoplait is a registered trademark of YOPLAIT MARQUES (France) used under license.

Cheerios First Birthday Cake

Prep Time: 45 Minutes • **Start to Finish:** 2 Hours • Makes 18 servings

1 box Betty Crocker Super-Moist yellow cake mix

1 cup mashed very ripe bananas (2 medium)

½ cup vegetable oil

¼ cup water

3 eggs

1 container (12 oz) Betty Crocker Whipped fluffy white frosting

1 cup Cheerios cereal

Cheerios, the familiar first food for babies, is a natural fit for a first birthday cake.

1 Heat oven to 350°F (325°F for dark or nonstick pans). Grease with shortening or cooking spray bottom only of 2 (6-inch) round cake pans, and place paper baking cup in each of 6 regular-size muffin cups.

2 In large bowl, beat cake mix, bananas, oil, water and eggs with electric mixer on low speed 30 seconds. Beat on medium speed 2 minutes, scraping bowl occasionally until smooth. Place 1¾ cups batter into each round cake pan. Divide remaining batter evenly among 6 lined muffin cups. Bake round cake 35 to 40 minutes and cupcakes 18 to 23 minutes or until toothpick inserted in cake comes out clean. Cool 10 minutes; remove from pans to cooling racks. Cool completely, about 30 minutes.

3 Slice 6-inch cake tops horizontally to remove rounded tops. Place 1 round cake cut side up on plate. Spread cut side with frosting. Top with remaining round cake, cut side down. Frost top and side of cake with frosting. Arrange cereal in single layer over top and side of cake. Place candle in top center of cake.

4 Use remaining frosting to frost cupcakes. Decorate with cereal, if desired.

1 Serving: Calories 260; Total Fat 12g (Saturated Fat 3g, Trans Fat 1g); Cholesterol 30mg; Sodium 210mg; Total Carbohydrate 36g (Dietary Fiber 0g); Protein 2g **Exchanges:** ½ Starch, 2 Other Carbohydrate, 2½ Fat **Carbohydrate Choices:** 2½

Tip If you don't have the 6-inch round cake pans, use 2 (8-inch) round cake pans. Divide the batter between pans. Bake 25 to 30 minutes. Make a paper template for a 6-inch circle. Place the template on each 8-inch cake layer and follow it to cut out 2 (6-inch) round cakes.

Rubber Ducky Cake

Prep Time: 30 Minutes • **Start to Finish:** 3 Hours 20 Minutes • Makes 15 servings

1 box Betty Crocker Super-Moist yellow cake mix

Water, vegetable oil and eggs called for on cake mix box

2 containers (12 oz each) Betty Crocker Whipped fluffy white frosting

Yellow food color

3 orange wedge candies

2 nonpareil candies (1-inch chocolate rounds topped with white sprinkles)

2 chocolate chips

1 Heat oven to 350°F (325°F for dark or nonstick pans). Grease or spray bottom and side of 1 (8-inch) round cake pan, 1 (9-inch) round cake pan and 1 (10-oz) custard cup.

2 Make cake batter as directed on box. Pour ⅔ cup batter into custard cup; divide remaining batter between cake pans. Bake 8-inch pan 21 to 26 minutes (dark or nonstick 25 to 30 minutes), 9-inch pan 17 to 23 minutes (dark or nonstick 20 to 26 minutes) and custard cup 21 to 26 minutes or until toothpick inserted in center comes out clean. Cool 10 minutes. Remove cakes from pans and custard cup; place rounded side up on cooling racks. Cool completely, about 30 minutes. Freeze cakes 45 minutes before cutting to reduce crumbs.

3 Spoon frosting into large bowl. Stir in enough food color until desired yellow color. Using serrated knife, cut rounded top off 8-inch cake. Place 8-inch cake cut side down on serving plate; spread ½ cup frosting over top. Place 9-inch cake rounded side up on frosted cake. Spread thin layer of frosting over side and top of layered cake to seal in crumbs. Freeze cake 30 to 60 minutes.

4 Reserve almost ⅔ cup frosting. Frost side and top of cake with remaining frosting. Place custard cup cake rounded side up 1 inch from edge of layered cake for head. Directly opposite head, place 2 orange candies side by side for tail shape. Frost head and candy tail with reserved frosting; place small dab of frosting on top of head with a slight "feather-like" curl, if desired.

5 Add nonpareil candies to head for eyes; add chocolate chips to centers of eyes, attaching with small amount of frosting. Cut rounded side of remaining orange candy to within ¼ inch of flat side. Using sugared fingers, press cut halves of candy to make them thin to form upper and lower halves of beak. Push 2 toothpicks through beak and insert under eyes. Remove toothpicks before serving. Store loosely covered.

1 Serving (Cake and Frosting Only): Calories 380; Total Fat 19g (Saturated Fat 5g, Trans Fat 3g); Cholesterol 40mg; Sodium 270mg; Total Carbohydrate 52g (Dietary Fiber 0g); Protein 2g **Exchanges:** ½ Starch, 3 Other Carbohydrate, 3½ Fat **Carbohydrate Choices:** 3½

Tip Create an attractive display by covering a piece of sturdy cardboard with wrapping paper, then plastic food wrap. Stretch and secure it with tape. Or cover the cardboard with foil or cooking parchment paper.

First Birthday Lion Cake

Prep Time: 40 Minutes • **Start to Finish:** 2 Hours • Makes 8 servings

- 1 box Betty Crocker Super-Moist yellow cake mix
- 1 cup mashed very ripe bananas (2 medium)
- ½ cup vegetable oil
- ¼ cup water
- 3 eggs
- 1 package (8 oz) cream cheese, softened
- 1 container (6 oz) Yoplait Original 99% Fat Free French vanilla yogurt
- Golden yellow gel or paste food color
- Orange gel or paste food color
- ¾ cup Cheerios cereal
- 6 pretzel sticks
- 2 brown candy-coated pieces
- Brown decorating gel

Capture first birthday moments with this cute cake that's filled with bananas, yogurt and Cheerios!

1. Heat oven to 350°F (325°F for dark or nonstick pans). Grease with shortening or cooking spray bottom only of 1 (6-inch) round cake pan, and place paper baking cup in each of 16 regular-size muffin cups.

2. In large bowl, beat cake mix, bananas, oil, water and eggs with electric mixer on low speed. Beat on medium speed 2 minutes, scraping bowl occasionally, until smooth. Place 1¾ cups batter in 6-inch round pan. Divide remaining batter evenly among 16 lined muffin cups. Bake round cake 35 to 40 minutes and cupcakes 18 to 23 minutes or until toothpick inserted in cake comes out clean. Cool 10 minutes; remove from pans to cooling racks. Cool completely, about 30 minutes.

3. In small bowl, beat cream cheese and yogurt on medium speed with electric mixer until creamy and smooth. Stir in yellow food color until mixture is desired color. In small bowl, place 3 tablespoons of yellow frosting; stir in orange food color until desired color.

4. Slice 6-inch round cake horizontally to remove rounded top. Place cake cut side down on plate. Use yellow frosting to frost top and side of cake. Use orange frosting to make muzzle. Place cereal around top edge of cake to make mane. Add brown candy-coated pieces for eyes. Insert pretzel sticks into cake near muzzle for whiskers. Use brown decorating gel to make mouth, nose and whisker spots on face.

5. Use remaining frosting to frost cupcakes. If desired, use additional cereal to decorate cupcakes. Store cake and cupcakes in refrigerator.

1 Serving: Calories 510; Total Fat 26g (Saturated Fat 9g, Trans Fat 0g); Cholesterol 100mg; Sodium 580mg; Total Carbohydrate 62g (Dietary Fiber nc); Protein nc **Exchanges:** ½ Starch, 3½ Other Carbohydrate, 1 Medium-Fat Meat, 4 Fat **Carbohydrate Choices:** 4

Tip If you don't have a 6-inch round cake pan, use an 8-inch round cake pan instead. Fill the pan with 2½ cups batter, and bake 25 to 30 minutes. Use the remaining batter to make 15 cupcakes. Make a paper template for a 6-inch circle. Place the template on the 8-inch cake and follow it to cut out a 6-inch round cake.

Balloon Fun Cake

Prep Time: 15 Minutes • **Start to Finish:** 2 Hours 35 Minutes • Makes 12 servings

- 2⅓ cups Gold Medal® all-purpose flour
- 1⅔ cups sugar
- ¾ cup butter or margarine, softened
- ⅔ cup unsweetened baking cocoa
- 1½ cups water
- 3½ teaspoons baking powder
- 1 teaspoon salt
- 3 eggs
- 1 container (12 oz) Betty Crocker whipped fluffy white frosting
- 5 coconut-covered marshmallow bon-bon cookies
- 6 pieces string licorice

Delight the kids with this beautiful baked balloon cake decorated with bon-bon cookies and string licorice over whipped fluffy white frosting.

1 Heat oven to 350°F. Grease bottom and sides of 13 x 9-inch pan with shortening; lightly flour.

2 In large bowl, beat all ingredients except frosting, cookies and licorice with electric mixer on low speed 30 seconds, scraping bowl constantly. Beat on high speed 3 minutes, scraping bowl occasionally. Pour into pan.

3 Bake 35 to 40 minutes or until toothpick inserted in center comes out clean. Cool 10 minutes; remove from pan to cooling rack. Cool completely, about 1 hour 30 minutes.

4 Spread frosting on top and sides of cake. Decorate with cookies and licorice to look like balloons on strings.

1 Serving: Calories 545; Total Fat 21g (Saturated Fat 9g, Trans Fat nc); Cholesterol 35mg; Sodium 370mg; Total Carbohydrate 86g (Dietary Fiber 2g); Protein 5g **Exchanges:** na **Carbohydrate Choices:** na

Tip Tint the frosting with blue food color to give the look of balloons floating across the sky.

Building Blocks Cakes

Prep Time: 35 Minutes • **Start to Finish:** 4 Hours 10 Minutes • Makes 12 servings

Building a birthday cake is fun and easy thanks to cake mix, ready-to-spread frosting and marshmallows.

1 Heat oven to 350°F (325°F for dark or nonstick pan). Grease or spray bottom and sides of 13 x 9-inch pan.

2 Make and bake cake mix as directed on box for 13 x 9-inch pan. Cool 10 minutes; remove from pan to cooling rack. Cool completely, about 1 hour. For easier handling, refrigerate or freeze cake about 1 hour or until firm.

3 Meanwhile, in small bowl for each color, tint 1 cup frosting red, 1 cup frosting yellow and ⅔ cup frosting blue with food colors. Leave remaining frosting white.

4 Using serrated knife, cut rounded dome from top of cake to make flat surface; place cake cut side down. Cut cake crosswise into thirds. Cut one of the thirds in half crosswise to make 2 squares. Place cake pieces on tray. (See photo.)

5 Spread top and sides of 1 square cake with thin layer of blue frosting and 1 square cake with thin layer of white frosting to seal in crumbs. Frost 1 rectangular cake with thin layer of yellow frosting and 1 rectangular cake with thin layer of red frosting. Refrigerate or freeze 30 to 60 minutes to set frosting.

6 Add final coat of frosting to each cake. Frost 4 marshmallow halves with blue frosting; place in square design on blue cake. Frost 4 marshmallow halves with white frosting; place in square design on white cake. Frost 8 marshmallow halves with yellow frosting; place on yellow cake. Frost 8 marshmallow halves with red frosting; place on red cake. Store loosely covered.

- 1 box Betty Crocker Super-Moist yellow cake mix
- Water, vegetable oil and eggs called for on cake mix box
- 2 containers (1 lb each) Betty Crocker Rich & Creamy vanilla frosting
- Red, yellow and blue gel or paste food colors
- Tray or cardboard (15 x 12 inches), covered with wrapping paper and plastic food wrap or foil
- 12 large marshmallows, cut in half crosswise

1 Serving: Calories 560; Total Fat 23g (Saturated Fat 5g, Trans Fat 4.5g); Cholesterol 55mg; Sodium 430mg; Total Carbohydrate 86g (Dietary Fiber 0g); Protein 2g **Exchanges:** ½ Starch, 5 Other Carbohydrate, 4½ Fat **Carbohydrate Choices:** 6

Tip Use kitchen scissors to cut the marshmallows. Spray the blades with cooking spray to keep them from getting sticky. Stick a fork in the side of the marshmallow half to hold it while frosting. Use a metal spatula or knife to slide the marshmallow from the fork onto the cake. Use a spatula to smooth the frosting on the marshmallow.

Favorite Animals

Inchworm Cake

Prep Time: 30 Minutes • **Start to Finish:** 2 Hours 30 Minutes • Makes 16 servings

- 1 box Betty Crocker Super-Moist cake mix (any flavor)
- Water, vegetable oil and eggs called for on cake mix box
- 8 drops green food color
- 1½ containers (1 lb each) Betty Crocker Rich & Creamy vanilla frosting
- Tray or cardboard (19 x 14 inches), covered with wrapping paper and plastic food wrap or foil
- 5 candy-coated chocolate candies
- 2 vanilla wafer cookies
- 2 small pretzel sticks
- 24 gumdrops

Inch your way into a fun celebration with an easy-to-make and fun-to-eat cake!

1 Heat oven to 350°F (325°F for dark or nonstick pan). Make, bake and cool cake as directed on box for 12-cup fluted tube cake pan.

2 Cut cake into 3 pieces for the body as shown in diagram 1. Freeze pieces uncovered 1 hour for easier frosting. Stir food color into frosting. Arrange cake pieces on tray to form inchworm as shown in diagram 2. Frost cake, attaching pieces with frosting.

3 Attach 1 chocolate candy to each vanilla wafer with frosting; attach to end of cake for eyes. Press 3 candies into frosting for mouth. Gently push 1 pretzel stick into flat end of gumdrop; repeat. Insert pretzel sticks into cake for antennae. Arrange remaining gumdrops along edge for feet. Store loosely covered.

1 Serving: Calories 340; Total Fat 15g (Saturated Fat 3g, Trans Fat 2.5g); Cholesterol 40mg; Sodium 290mg; Total Carbohydrate 51g (Dietary Fiber 0g); Protein 1g **Exchanges:** ½ Starch, 3 Other Carbohydrate, 3 Fat **Carbohydrate Choices:** 3½

Tip Paste food color will produce more vividly colored frosting than the liquid type.

Cutting and Assembling Inchworm Cake

1. Cut cake into three pieces for the body.

2. Arrange pieces on tray to form inchworm.

Dinosaur Cake

Prep Time: 30 Minutes • **Start to Finish:** 3 Hours 45 Minutes • Makes 15 servings

1 box Betty Crocker SuperMoist yellow or devil's food cake mix

1 cup water

½ cup vegetable oil

3 eggs

Tray or cardboard (18 x 14 inches), covered with wrapping paper and plastic food wrap or foil

2 containers (1 lb each) Betty Crocker Rich & Creamy vanilla frosting

Green gel food color

Assorted yellow round candies (candy-coated chocolate candies, candy coating wafers, chewy round candies)

Chocolate chips

Calling all dinosaur lovers. Celebrate with a foolproof cake decorated with bright candies — what fun!

1 Heat oven to 350°F (325°F for dark or nonstick pans). Grease or spray 2 (8- or 9-inch) round cake pans. In large bowl, beat cake mix, water, oil and eggs with electric mixer on low speed 30 seconds, then on medium speed 2 minutes, scraping bowl occasionally. Divide batter between pans. Bake and cool cake as directed on box for 8- or 9-inch rounds. For easier handling, freeze cake 45 minutes or until firm.

2 Cut 1 cake in half lengthwise, making 2 half-rounds. Sculpt 1 half-round into a head and the other half-round into a tail. For body, cut 1-inch slice from edge of remaining whole cake. From cut edge, cut out small inverted U-shaped piece. Place body on tray; arrange head and tail pieces next to body as shown in diagrams 1 and 2.

3 Spoon frosting into large bowl. Stir in enough food color until desired green color. Attach cake pieces with a small amount of frosting. Spread thin layer of frosting over entire cake to seal in crumbs. Refrigerate or freeze cake 30 to 60 minutes to set frosting. Frost entire cake.

4 Decorate with yellow candies. Add chocolate chips for eyes. Store loosely covered.

1 Serving (Cake and Frosting Only): Calories 390; Total Fat 16g (Saturated Fat 3.5g, Trans Fat 3.5g); Cholesterol 35mg; Sodium 300mg; Total Carbohydrate 59g (Dietary Fiber 0g); Protein 1g **Exchanges:** ½ Starch, 3½ Other Carbohydrate, 3 Fat **Carbohydrate Choices:** 4

Tip Use a variety of candies to make your dino come alive. Create a patch of grass for your dino by coloring coconut with green food color. Sprinkle it around the dino's feet.

Cutting and Assembling Dinosaur Cake

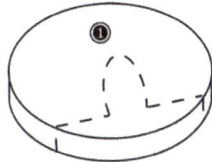

1. Cut 9-inch cake for the body.

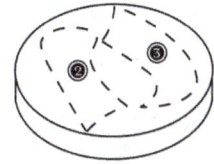

2. Cut 9-inch cake for the head and tail.

3. Arrange pieces on tray to form dinosaur.

Favorite Animals

Easy Bunny Cakes

Prep Time: 30 Minutes • **Start to Finish:** 2 Hours 10 Minutes • Makes 16 servings

Hop into creating the easiest pair of bunny birthday cakes you'll ever make.

1 Heat oven to 350°F (325°F for dark or nonstick pans). Make, bake and cool cake as directed on box for 2 (8-inch or 9-inch) round cake pans.

2 In medium bowl, tint 1 container frosting with neon purple food color. Using 1 cake round, cut in half to form 2 half-rounds. Put halves together with ¼ cup frosting to form body. Place upright on serving plate, cut side down.

3 Frost cake with frosting. Cut ears from construction paper; wrap ends that will be inserted into cake with plastic food wrap. Insert into cake. Using toothpicks to attach, use 2 small marshmallow halves and 2 small jelly bean halves for eyes. Use large jelly bean for nose and sour candy strips for whiskers. Place gum halves just below nose for teeth. Use large marshmallow for tail. (See photo.)

4 Repeat with remaining cake to make second bunny, using neon pink food color. Frost and decorate as above. Remove ears, plastic wrap and toothpicks before serving. Store loosely covered.

- 1 box Betty Crocker Super-Moist yellow cake mix
- Water, vegetable oil and eggs called for on cake mix box
- 2 containers (1 lb each) Betty Crocker Rich & Creamy vanilla frosting
- Neon purple and/or pink food color
- Construction paper (inedible)
- 2 small marshmallows, cut in half, flattened
- 2 small jelly beans, cut in half
- 2 (5-inch) strips rainbow-colored sour candy, separated into strips
- 2 large jelly beans or candy-coated chocolate-covered peanut candies
- 2 pieces rectangular-shaped white chewing gum, cut in half
- 2 large marshmallows

1 Serving (Cake and Frosting Only): Calories 400; Total Fat 17g (Saturated Fat 3.5g, Trans Fat 3.5g); Cholesterol 40mg; Sodium 320mg; Total Carbohydrate 60g (Dietary Fiber 0g); Protein 1g **Exchanges:** ½ Starch, 3½ Other Carbohydrate, 3½ Fat **Carbohydrate Choices:** 4

Tip Give your bunnies some grass to sit in. Color shredded coconut by shaking it with a few drops of green food color in a resealable food-storage plastic bag.

Pull-Apart Turtle Cupcakes

Prep Time: 30 Minutes • **Start to Finish:** 2 Hours • Makes 24 cupcakes (2 turtles)

1 box Betty Crocker SuperMoist yellow or devil's food cake mix

Water, vegetable oil and eggs called for on cake mix box

1 container (1 lb) Betty Crocker Rich & Creamy vanilla frosting

Green food color

1 container (1 lb) Betty Crocker Rich & Creamy chocolate frosting

4 green candy-coated chocolate candies

4 brown miniature candy-coated chocolate candies, if desired

1 piece red string licorice

1 green licorice twist, cut in half

What a clever way to make a birthday cake! Just arrange the cupcakes in the shape of a turtle, frost and decorate.

1 Heat oven to 350°F (325°F for dark or nonstick pans). Place paper baking cup in each of 24 regular-size muffin cups. Make and bake cake mix as directed on box for 24 cupcakes. Cool 10 minutes; remove from pans to cooling racks. Cool completely, about 30 minutes.

2 In small bowl, mix vanilla frosting and green food color until desired shade. Place ¼ cup green frosting and ¼ cup chocolate frosting in separate small resealable freezer plastic bags; seal bags. Cut small tip off 1 corner of each bag; set aside.

3 On each of 2 large serving trays, arrange 12 cupcakes as shown in photo to resemble turtle. Frost shell of 1 turtle with chocolate frosting. Frost head and feet with green frosting. (Push cupcakes together slightly to frost entire turtle, not just individual cupcakes.) Pipe green frosting on chocolate shell to create turtle design. Add 2 candies for eyes; add pupils using chocolate frosting. Add nostrils with chocolate frosting or miniature chocolate candies. Add red string licorice for mouth (trimming to fit) and green licorice for tail.

4 Frost remaining cupcakes with green frosting for shell and chocolate frosting for head and feet. Pipe chocolate frosting on green shell to create turtle design. Add 2 candies for eyes; add pupils using chocolate frosting. Add nostrils with green frosting or miniature chocolate candies. Add red string licorice for mouth (trimming to fit) and green licorice for tail. Store loosely covered.

1 Cupcake (Cake and Frosting Only): Calories 260; Total Fat 11g (Saturated Fat 2.5g, Trans Fat 2g); Cholesterol 25mg; Sodium 230mg; Total Carbohydrate 39g (Dietary Fiber 0g); Protein 1g **Exchanges:** ½ Starch, 2 Other Carbohydrate, 2 Fat **Carbohydrate Choices:** 2½

Tip If you have only 1 pan and a recipe calls for more cupcakes than your pan will make, cover and refrigerate the rest of the batter while baking the first batch. Cool the pan about 15 minutes, then bake the rest of the batter, adding 1 to 2 minutes to the bake time.

Pony Cake

Prep Time: 1 Hour 30 Minutes • **Start to Finish:** 4 Hours 30 Minutes • Makes 12 servings

- 1 box Betty Crocker SuperMoist yellow or devil's food cake mix
- 1 cup water
- ½ cup vegetable oil
- 3 eggs
- 1 container (1 lb) Betty Crocker Rich & Creamy vanilla frosting
- Red food color
- 1 container (1 lb) Betty Crocker Rich & Creamy chocolate frosting
- Tray or cardboard (20 x 15 inches), covered with wrapping paper and plastic food wrap or foil
- 1 small round chocolate-covered creamy mint

Giddyup! It's time for a birthday party, and this pony cake is big enough to corral a bunch of kids.

1 Heat oven to 350°F (325°F for dark or nonstick pans). Grease or spray 2 (9-inch) round cake pans. In large bowl, beat cake mix, water, oil and eggs with electric mixer on low speed 30 seconds, then on medium speed 2 minutes, scraping bowl occasionally. Divide batter between pans. Bake as directed on box for 9-inch rounds. Cool 10 minutes; remove from pans to cooling racks. Cool completely, about 30 minutes. For easier handling, refrigerate or freeze cakes 30 to 60 minutes or until firm.

2 Meanwhile, in small bowl, tint ¼ cup vanilla frosting with red food color to make pink; place in resealable freezer plastic bag. Place ½ cup chocolate frosting in another resealable freezer plastic bag. Cut small tip off 1 corner of each bag. In medium bowl, stir together remaining vanilla frosting and chocolate frosting to make light brown frosting.

3 Using serrated knife, cut off rounded portion of top of each cake to make level. Turn cakes cut side down. Cut cakes as shown in diagrams 1 and 2. On tray, arrange cake pieces as shown in diagram 3, attaching pieces to each other and to tray with small amount of light brown frosting. Spread thin layer of light brown frosting over entire cake to seal in crumbs. Refrigerate or freeze cake 30 to 60 minutes to set frosting.

4 Frost entire cake with light brown frosting. With pink frosting, pipe on blanket; spread with metal spatula to make smooth. With darker chocolate frosting, pipe number on blanket. Pipe on hooves; spread to make smooth. Pipe on mane and tail, leaving in long strands to look like hair. Attach mint for eye. Store loosely covered.

1 Serving (Cake and Frosting Only): Calories 440; Total Fat 19g (Saturated Fat 4.5g, Trans Fat 4.5g); Cholesterol 35mg; Sodium 360mg; Total Carbohydrate 68g (Dietary Fiber 0g); Protein 1g **Exchanges:** 1 Starch, 3½ Other Carbohydrate, 3½ Fat **Carbohydrate Choices:** 4½

Cutting and Assembling Pony Cake

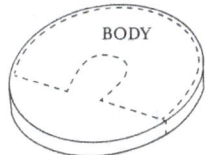
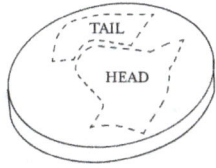
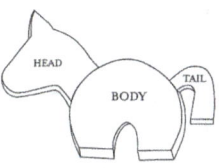

1. Cut 9-inch cake for the body.

2. Cut 9-inch cake for the head and tail.

3. Arrange pieces on tray to form pony.

Favorite Animals · **19**

Panda Bear Cake

Prep Time: 1 Hour 30 Minutes • **Start to Finish:** 4 Hours 30 Minutes • Makes 20 servings

- 2 boxes Betty Crocker SuperMoist devil's food or yellow cake mix
- 2 cups water
- 1 cup vegetable oil
- 6 eggs
- 1½ containers (1 lb each) Betty Crocker Rich & Creamy chocolate frosting
- Black food color
- 1 large marshmallow
- 2 small round chocolate-covered creamy mints
- Tray or cardboard (20 x 18 inches), covered with wrapping paper and plastic food wrap or foil
- 1½ containers (1 lb each) Betty Crocker Rich & Creamy vanilla frosting

Party time! Create a sweet panda to celebrate a birthday.

1 Heat oven to 350°F (325°F for dark or nonstick pans). Grease bottoms and sides of 2 (8-inch) round cake pans and 1 (13 x 9-inch) pan, or spray with baking spray with flour. In large bowl, beat 1 cake mix, 1 cup of the water, ½ cup of the oil and 3 of the eggs with electric mixer on low speed 30 seconds, then on medium speed 2 minutes, scraping bowl occasionally. Divide batter between round pans. Bake as directed on box for 8-inch round pan. Cool 10 minutes; remove from pans to cooling racks. In large bowl, beat remaining cake mix, remaining 1 cup water, remaining ½ cup oil and remaining 3 eggs with electric mixer on low speed 30 seconds, then on medium speed 2 minutes, stirring occasionally. Pour into 13 x 9-inch pan. Bake as directed on box for 13 x 9-inch pan. Cool 10 minutes; remove from pan to cooling rack. Cool completely, about 1 hour. For easier handling, refrigerate or freeze cakes about 1 hour or until firm.

2 Meanwhile, in medium bowl, mix 1 container plus 1 cup chocolate frosting with food color to make black frosting. Cut marshmallow in half crosswise.

3 Using serrated knife, cut off top rounded portion of each cake to level surface. Turn cakes cut side down. Set aside one 8-inch cake for head. Cut remaining cakes as shown in diagrams 1 and 2. Place cake pieces on tray as shown in diagram 3, attaching to tray and to each other with small amount of frosting.

4 Spread thin layer of vanilla frosting over head and thin layer of black frosting over ears, body and paws to seal in crumbs. Refrigerate or freeze cake 30 to 60 minutes to set frosting.

5 Frost head with some of remaining vanilla frosting. Frost rest of cake with some of remaining black frosting. Spoon vanilla and black frostings into separate resealable freezer plastic bags; cut small tip off 1 corner of each bag.

6 Pipe or spread vanilla frosting on body to create chest. Pipe or spread black frosting on head for patches around eyes. Place marshmallow eyes on patches. For pupils, attach 1 mint to each marshmallow slice with frosting. Pipe or spread black frosting on snout for nose and mouth. Pipe or spread vanilla frosting on back paws to create paw prints. Pipe outline around body and front legs with black frosting. Fill in outline with additional black frosting so front legs have a thicker layer of frosting than white chest. Using metal spatula, create a different texture on the body and front legs to further define legs from chest and back paws. Store loosely covered.

1 Serving (Cake and Frosting Only): Calories 540; Total Fat 24g (Saturated Fat 6g, Trans Fat 4g); Cholesterol 65mg; Sodium 540mg; Total Carbohydrate 78g (Dietary Fiber 1g); Protein 4g **Exchanges:** 1½ Starch, 3½ Other Carbohydrate, 4½ Fat **Carbohydrate Choices:** 5

Tip This panda can easily be frosted to create any type of bear. Frost with different shades of brown to create a cuddly brown bear. For a polar bear, frost with white frosting, then accent with grays and black.

Cutting and Assembling Panda Bear Cake

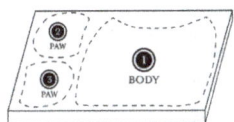

1. Cut 13 x 9-inch cake for the body and paws.

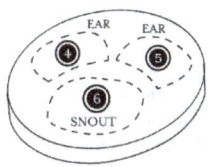

2. Cut second 8-inch cake for the ears and snout.

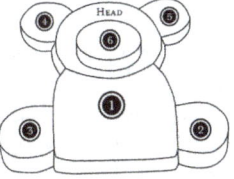

3. Arrange pieces on tray to form panda.

Favorite Animals · 21

Barn Cake with Farm Animal Cupcakes

Prep Time: 1 Hour 35 Minutes • **Start to Finish:** 4 Hours 45 Minutes • Makes 20 servings

Cake, Cupcakes and Frosting

- 1 box Betty Crocker SuperMoist yellow or devil's food cake mix
- Water, vegetable oil and eggs called for on cake mix box
- 2 containers (1 lb each) Betty Crocker Rich & Creamy vanilla frosting
- Red liquid food color
- Red gel or paste food color

Barn Decorations

- Tray or cardboard (20 x 15 inches), covered with wrapping paper and plastic food wrap or foil
- 5 thin pretzel sticks
- 6 graham cracker squares
- 1½ cups shredded coconut
- Yellow liquid food color
- Green liquid food color

Chick Decorations

- Reserved yellow coconut (from barn)
- 8 brown miniature candy-coated chocolate baking bits
- 4 small orange gumdrops

Sheep Decorations

- 4 red miniature candy-coated chocolate baking bits
- 8 brown miniature candy-coated chocolate baking bits
- 4 small white gumdrops, cut in half vertically
- 64 miniature marshmallows, cut in half crosswise

Pig Decorations

- 8 red miniature candy-coated chocolate baking bits
- 8 brown miniature candy-coated chocolate baking bits
- 1 roll Betty Crocker Fruit Roll-Ups® strawberry chewy fruit snack (from 5-oz box)

Bake up a delicious red barn and fun-to-decorate animals.

1 Heat oven to 350°F (325°F for dark or nonstick pans). Grease or spray bottom and sides of 9-inch square pan. Place paper baking cup in each of 12 regular-size muffin cups. Make cake batter as directed on box. Pour 2¼ cups batter into square pan; divide remaining batter evenly among muffin cups. Bake yellow cupcakes 15 to 20 minutes and yellow square pan 20 to 26 minutes) OR devil's food cupcakes 18 to 23 minutes and devil's food square pan 21 to 28 minutes or until toothpick inserted in centers comes out clean. Cool 10 minutes; remove from pans to cooling racks. Cool completely, about 30 minutes. For easier handling, refrigerate or freeze square cake 30 to 60 minutes or until firm.

2 In small bowl, tint 1 cup of the frosting with red liquid food color to make pink frosting. In medium bowl, tint 1½ cups of the frosting with red gel or paste food color to make desired color of red frosting for barn; set aside. Reserve remaining white frosting. Decorate square cake to make barn (step 3); decorate cupcakes to make 4 chicks, 4 sheep and 4 pigs (steps 4, 5 and 6).

3 Barn: Trim 1 side of square cake to form roof of barn; place cake near top of tray with roof at top of tray. (See photo.) Spread thin layer of red frosting over entire cake to seal in crumbs. Refrigerate or freeze cake 30 to 60 minutes. Frost sides and top of cake with remaining red frosting. Using spatula or toothpick, make vertical lines on top of cake to look like boards.

- For window, break 2 pretzel sticks in half; place near top of cake in square shape.
- For shutters, place 1-inch-square piece of graham cracker on each side of window.
- For sides and top of doorway, place 3 pretzel sticks near bottom of cake.
- For doors, place 2½ x 1-inch graham cracker rectangle on each side of doorway.
- For roof, arrange 8 (2½ x 1-inch) graham cracker rectan-

gles on top edge of cake, overlapping to form barn roof shape.

- For hay, place ½ cup of the coconut in resealable food-storage plastic bag. Add 2 drops yellow liquid food color; seal bag and shake to mix. Place small amount of yellow coconut at bottom of window and doorway (reserve remaining yellow coconut to decorate chick cupcakes).

- For grass, place remaining 1 cup coconut in resealable food-storage plastic bag. Add 2 drops green liquid food color; seal bag and shake to mix. Scatter green coconut on bottom half of tray. Decorate cupcakes and arrange on coconut grass.

4 **Chicks:** Frost 4 cupcakes with white frosting. Top with reserved yellow coconut. For eyes, add brown baking bits. Cut orange gumdrops to look like beaks; place on cupcakes.

5 **Sheep:** Frost 4 cupcakes with white frosting. For muzzle, spread ½ teaspoon pink frosting in small circle on each cupcake; add red baking bit for nose. For eyes, add brown baking bits. For ears, add white gumdrop halves, cut side down. Place marshmallow halves on face for wool.

6 **Pigs:** Frost 4 cupcakes with pink frosting. For snout, spread additional 1 teaspoon pink frosting in small circle on each cupcake; add red baking bits for nostrils. For eyes, add brown baking bits. For ears, cut 8 small triangles from fruit snack; place on cupcakes. Store loosely covered.

1 Serving (Cake and Frosting Only): Calories 320; Total Fat 13g (Saturated Fat 3g, Trans Fat 2.5g); Cholesterol 30mg; Sodium 260mg; Total Carbohydrate 48g (Dietary Fiber 0g); Protein 1g **Exchanges:** ½ Starch, 2½ Other Carbohydrate, 2½ Fat **Carbohydrate Choices:** 3

Theme Parties

Little Car Cakes

Prep Time: 30 Minutes • **Start to Finish:** 3 Hours 10 Minutes • Makes 12 servings

1 box Betty Crocker Super-Moist yellow cake mix

Water, vegetable oil and eggs called for on cake mix box

Large tray or cardboard (20 x 15) covered with wrapping paper and plastic food wrap or foil

2 containers (1 lb each) Betty Crocker Rich & Creamy vanilla frosting

Blue, red, green and yellow food colors

Red or black string licorice

8 yellow round starlight candies

10 creme-filled chocolate sandwich cookies

1 red or orange gumdrop

2 birthday cake candles

1 Heat oven to 350°F (325°F for dark or nonstick pans). Grease bottoms only of 3 (8 x 4-inch) loaf pans, or spray bottoms with cooking spray.

2 Make cake batter as directed on cake mix box. Divide batter evenly among pans.

3 Bake 25 to 32 minutes (28 to 37 minutes for dark or nonstick pans) or until toothpick inserted in center comes out clean. Cool 10 minutes. Run knife around sides of pans to loosen cakes; remove from pans to cooling rack. Cool completely, about 1 hour. Freeze cakes uncovered about 1 hour for easier frosting.

4 Remove ¼ cup frosting from each container and place in small bowls; set aside. To make purple frosting, stir 8 drops blue food color and 8 drops red food color into 1 container frosting. To make bright green frosting, stir 3 drops green food color and 3 drops yellow food color into other container frosting.

5 Place 2 loaves, rounded side down, on tray. To seal in crumbs, spread top and sides of 1 cake with thin layer of purple frosting; frost second cake with thin layer of green frosting. Cut remaining loaf crosswise in half; taper the cut edges slightly to form windshields. Place 1 half on each cake for cab, placing about 3 inches from front edge and with tapered windshield side toward front of car. Frost windows of cabs with a thin layer of reserved vanilla frosting; frost top and edges with a thin layer of colored frosting. (See photo.) Refrigerate or freeze cakes 30 to 60 minutes to set frosting. Frost entire cars with same colors.

6 Use licorice to outline windows and make bumpers. Add starlight candies for headlights and taillights; add cookies for wheels and the spares. Place gumdrop on top of 1 car for beacon and add candles for radio antennas. Store loosely covered.

1 Serving: Calories 530; Total Fat 22g (Saturated Fat 5g, Trans Fat 4.5g); Cholesterol 55mg; Sodium 430mg; Total Carbohydrate 80g (Dietary Fiber 0g); Protein 2g **Exchanges:** ½ Starch, 5 Other Carbohydrate, 4½ Fat **Carbohydrate Choices:** 5

Beary Fun Cupcake Cones

Prep Time: 20 Minutes • **Start to Finish:** 2 Hours 35 Minutes • Makes 30 to 36 cupcake cones

1 box Betty Crocker Super-Moist cake mix (any flavor)

Water, vegetable oil and eggs called for on cake mix box

30 to 36 flat-bottom ice cream cones

1 container (12 oz) Betty Crocker Whipped frosting (any white variety)

Assorted candies and decorations, if desired

Make a big splash with sweet cupcakes that bake right inside the cones!

1 Heat oven to 350°F (325°F for dark or nonstick pans). Make cake batter as directed on box. Fill each of 12 cones about half full of batter. Stand cones in muffin pan. Refrigerate any leftover batter until ready to fill and bake remaining cones. (Yield for different cake mix flavors will vary from 30 to 36 cupcake cones.)

2 Bake 21 to 26 minutes or until toothpick carefully inserted in center comes out clean. Cool completely, about 1 hour.

3 Frost with frosting and decorate. Store loosely covered.

1 Cupcake Cone: Calories 160; Total Fat 7g (Saturated Fat 2g, Trans Fat 1g); Cholesterol 20mg; Sodium 125mg; Total Carbohydrate 22g (Dietary Fiber 0g); Protein 1g **Exchanges:** ½ Starch, 1 Other Carbohydrate, 1 ½ Fat **Carbohydrate Choices:** 1 ½

Tip Tint the frosting blue for water, and use teddy bear–shaped graham snacks for "people." Add gummy candy rings for inner tubes, gumballs for beach balls and striped gum for inflatable floats. Help steady the cupcake cones on a serving plate by putting a small amount of frosting on the cone bottom, then lightly press the cone onto the plate.

Fire Engine Cake

Prep Time: 1 Hour 20 Minutes • **Start to Finish:** 3 Hours 5 Minutes • Makes 12 servings

Cake

- 1 box Betty Crocker SuperMoist devil's food or yellow cake mix
- Water, vegetable oil and eggs called for on cake mix box
- Platter, tray or cardboard (14 x 10 inches), covered with wrapping paper and plastic food wrap or foil

Frosting and Decorations

- 2 containers (1 lb each) Betty Crocker Rich & Creamy vanilla frosting
- Black food color
- Red gel or paste food color
- 10 red chewy fruit-flavored gumdrops (not sugar coated)
- 6 yellow chewy fruit-flavored gumdrops (not sugar coated)
- 4 creme-filled chocolate sandwich cookies
- 2 pieces black licorice coil

Create four-alarm birthday excitement with a fire engine cake! It's not only fun to make but fun to eat too.

1. Heat oven to 350°F (325°F for dark or nonstick pans). Grease or spray bottoms and sides of 3 (8 x 4-inch) loaf pans.

2. Make cake batter as directed on box. Divide batter evenly among pans. Bake 27 to 34 minutes or until toothpick inserted in center comes out clean. Cool 10 minutes. Remove from pans; place rounded side up on cooling racks. Cool completely, about 1 hour.

3. Spoon ½ cup of the frosting into small bowl; stir in enough black food color to make gray. Place ½ cup of the remaining white vanilla frosting in small resealable food-storage plastic bag; cut small tip off 1 corner of bag. Spoon remaining white vanilla frosting into large bowl; stir in enough red food color until desired red color.

4. Trim rounded tops from each cake to make flat surface. Place 1 cake on platter to form base as in diagram 1. Cut remaining cakes as shown in diagrams 2 and 3. Place cake pieces on platter as shown in diagram 4, attaching pieces with thin layer of red frosting, to form fire engine. Spread thin layer of red frosting over entire cake to seal in crumbs. For easier handling, refrigerate or freeze cake 30 to 60 minutes.

5. Frost area between cab and back of engine with gray frosting. Place remaining gray frosting in small resealable freezer plastic bag; cut small tip off 1 corner of bag. Frost remaining fire engine with red frosting. Pipe on windshield, windows and ladder with white frosting. Trim off and discard thin slice (about ⅛ inch) from bottoms of 4 red and 4 yellow gumdrops; attach trimmed gumdrops for headlights and taillights with white frosting. Attach remaining gumdrops on top of engine for lights. For wheels, pipe ½-inch circle of gray frosting on center of each cookie for hubcap; attach wheels to cake. Attach licorice coils on sides of cake for hoses.

6. Pipe gray frosting around wheels and bottom edge of engine. For bumpers, pipe 1 or 2 lines of gray frosting on front and back of engine. Store loosely covered.

1 Serving (Cake and Frosting Only): Calories 530; Total Fat 22g (Saturated Fat 5g, Trans Fat 4.5g); Cholesterol 55mg; Sodium 470mg; Total Carbohydrate 79g (Dietary Fiber 0g); Protein 3g **Exchanges:** ½ Starch, 5 Other Carbohydrate, 4½ Fat **Carbohydrate Choices:** 5

Tip Do you need to bake the cake in batches? Just cover and refrigerate batter in the mixing bowl while the first batch is baking. An extra minute or two for baking the second batch may be needed.

Cutting and Assembling Fire Engine Cake

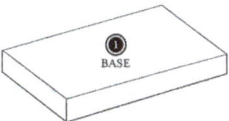

1. Place one 8 x 4-inch cake on serving tray for base.

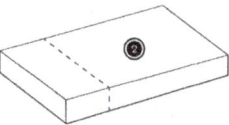

2. Cut 2 inches off one end of second 8 x 4-inch cake.

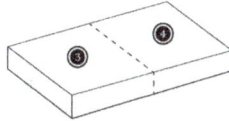

3. Cut third 8 x 4-inch cake in half.

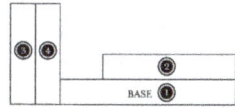

4. Arrange pieces to form fire engine.

Theme Parties · 27

Party-Time Purse Cake

Prep Time: 40 minutes • **Start to Finish:** 3 hours • Makes 15 servings

Cake

1 box white cake mix with pudding

Water, vegetable oil and egg whites called for on cake mix box

Frosting and Decorations

1½ containers (1 lb each) Betty Crocker Rich & Creamy creamy white frosting

Blue paste food color

1 plastic plate

1 or 2 large marshmallows

Colored sugar

Candy-coated chocolate candies

1 Heat oven to 350°F (325°F for dark or nonstick pan). Make, bake and cool cake as directed on box for 13 x 9-inch pan.

2 Cut cake crosswise in half as shown in diagram 1. On serving plate, place 1 cake piece; spread top with 2 tablespoons white frosting from ½ container. Top with second cake piece. Stand cake pieces on end with cut sides down as shown in diagram 2. Freeze 1 hour.

3 Stir food color into 1 container of frosting to tint light blue. Spread entire cake with light blue frosting as shown in diagram 3.

4 Along front and top of cake, mark outline of an elongated V-shape with toothpick for purse flap as shown in diagram 4. Stir food color into remaining ½ container of frosting to tint dark blue; frost purse flap with dark blue frosting. Place remaining dark blue frosting in decorating bag fitted with writing tip #7 or #8; pipe shell border along purse flap and edges of purse.

5 Cut rim from plastic plate; cut rim in half. Insert into top of cake for handle. Decorate purse with candies. Cut marshmallow with dampened kitchen scissors into slices; sprinkle with colored sugar. Arrange marshmallow slices on purse for clasp. Press candy onto center of clasp. Store loosely covered.

1 Serving (Cake and Frosting Only): Calories 350; Total Fat 13g (Saturated Fat 3g; Trans Fat 2.5g); Cholesterol 0mg; Sodium 320mg; Total Carbohydrate 56g (Dietary Fiber 0g); Protein 2g **Exchanges:** ½ Starch, 3 Other Carbohydrate, 2½ Fat **Carbohydrate Choices:** 4

Tip Choose from the many colorful candies available to decorate this adorable cake.

Cutting and Assembling Party-Time Purse Cake

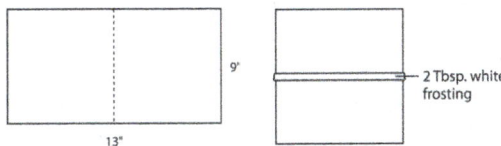

1. Cut cake crosswise in half.

2. Stand cake pieces on end with cut sides down.

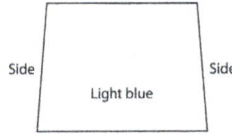
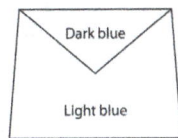

3. Spread cake with light blue frosting.

4. Mark V-shape with toothpick for purse flap.

Theme Parties · 29

Mermaid Cake

Prep Time: 1 Hour 10 Minutes • **Start to Finish:** 2 Hours 50 Minutes • Makes 12 servings

- 1 box Betty Crocker Super-Moist yellow cake mix
- Water, vegetable oil and eggs called for on cake mix box
- 1½ containers (1 lb each) Betty Crocker Rich & Creamy vanilla frosting
- Blue food color
- 1 tablespoon purple colored sugar
- 1 tablespoon blue colored sugar
- 1 fashion doll in swimsuit or sleeveless top (11½ inches tall)
- 3 rolls Betty Crocker Fruit Roll-Ups chewy fruit snack (from 5-oz box)
- Granulated sugar
- 6 large orange, yellow and/or white gumdrops
- 8 assorted sea creature candies

1. Heat oven to 350°F (325°F for dark or nonstick pans). Grease or spray bottoms and sides of 1 (10-oz) custard cup and 2 (8-inch) round cake pans.

2. Make cake batter as directed on box. Pour ⅔ cup batter into custard cup; divide remaining cake batter between cake pans. Bake 23 to 28 minutes (26 to 33 minutes for dark or nonstick pans) or until toothpick inserted in centers comes out clean. Cool 10 minutes. Remove cakes from custard cup and pans; place rounded side up on cooling racks. Cool completely, about 1 hour.

3. Trim off rounded tops from 8-inch cakes to make flat surfaces. On serving plate, place 1 round cake layer cut side down. Spread with ⅓ cup of the frosting. Top with second round cake layer cut side down. Trim off rounded top of custard-cup cake to make flat surface. With small amount of frosting, attach custard-cup cake, flat side down, to top of layer cake, lining up rounded edge with layer cake edge. Using doll as a guide, cut and remove rounded piece from custard-cup cake to make seat for doll. (Discard cut-out piece.)

4. Into small bowl, spoon ¾ cup of the frosting. Tint with blue food color to make light blue; set aside. Frost top and sides of cake with remaining white frosting. To add waves, frost lower side of cake with blue frosting. Dip a fork in a few drops additional blue food color; swirl in blue frosting on cake to add wave effect. Sprinkle top of cake with colored sugars.

5. Tie hair of fashion doll in ponytail. (Keep swimsuit or clothes on doll.) Wrap body of doll with plastic wrap, covering chest and leaving arms free and shoulders uncovered. With 2 fruit snack rolls, wrap plastic-wrapped portion of doll, overlapping rolls and pressing to stick together. Wrap third snack roll around legs and extend 2 inches beyond feet; press together to form a fin shape, trimming if necessary. Place doll in seat on cake.

6 To make starfish, on surface sprinkled with granulated sugar, flatten each gumdrop to make 1½-inch round. Using scissors, cut 5 wedges from each gumdrop round to form a star. Pull gently to extend points of stars. Decorate cake and serving plate with starfish and sea creature candies. Store loosely covered.

1 Serving (Cake and Frosting Only): Calories 460; Total Fat 20g (Saturated Fat 4.5g, Trans Fat 3.5g); Cholesterol 55mg; Sodium 390mg; Total Carbohydrate 68g (Dietary Fiber 0g); Protein 2g **Exchanges:** ½ Starch, 4 Other Carbohydrate, 4 Fat **Carbohydrate Choices:** 4½

Tip Place Fruit Roll-Ups snack rolls in the refrigerator for a few minutes to help release them from the plastic wrapper, if necessary.

Fairy Tale Princess Cake

Prep Time: 40 Minutes • **Start to Finish:** 3 Hours 40 Minutes • Makes 30 servings

2 boxes Betty Crocker SuperMoist yellow cake mix

Water, vegetable oil and eggs called for on cake mix boxes

3 containers (1 lb each) Betty Crocker Rich & Creamy vanilla frosting

Red food color

1 fashion doll (11½ inches tall)

¼ cup star-shaped candy sprinkles

Delight your princess with a magical cake that's made foolproof with an easy cake mix and purchased frosting.

1. Heat oven to 325°F. Grease a 1½-quart ovenproof bowl (8 inches across top) and 3 (8-inch) round cake pans with shortening; coat with flour (do not use cooking spray).

2. In large bowl, make both cake mixes as directed on boxes. (Two boxes of cake mix can be made at one time; do not make more than 2 boxes, and do not increase beating time.) Pour 3¼ cups batter into 1½-quart bowl, and divide remaining batter evenly among 3 pans (almost 2 cups batter into each cake pan).

3. Bake cake pans 23 to 30 minutes and bowl 47 to 53 minutes or until toothpick inserted in center comes out clean. Cool 10 minutes. Remove cakes from pans and bowl; place rounded side up on cooling racks. Cool completely, about 1 hour. Freeze cake 45 minutes. If necessary, cut off rounded tops of cakes to create flat surfaces. Cut bowl cake in half horizontally. Cut 2-inch-diameter hole in center of all 5 cake layers.

4. Spoon frosting into large bowl. Stir in enough food color until desired pink color. Place one 8-inch cake on serving plate; spread ⅓ cup frosting over top. Top with second 8-inch cake; spread with ⅓ cup frosting. Repeat with third layer; top with larger bowl cake layer cut side up. Spread with a small amount of frosting. Top with rounded bowl cake layer cut side down. Trim side of cake if necessary to make a tapered "skirt."

5. Spread thin layer of frosting over side and top of layered cake to seal in crumbs. Freeze cake 30 to 45 minutes to set frosting.

6. Wrap hair and lower half of doll with plastic wrap. Insert doll into center of cake.

7 Fit #24 star tip into decorating bag. Spoon ¼ cup pink frosting into decorating bag; set aside. Starting at waist of doll, frost cake with downward strokes to make ruffled skirt. Use star tip to cover bodice of doll and add decoration to skirt if desired. Gently press star candies into frosting to decorate neckline and skirt. Unwrap hair. Store cake loosely covered.

1 Serving (Cake and Frosting Only): Calories 370; Total Fat 16g (Saturated Fat 3.5g, Trans Fat 2.5g); Cholesterol 40mg; Sodium 310mg; Total Carbohydrate 56g (Dietary Fiber 0g); Protein 2g **Exchanges:** ½ Starch, 3 Other Carbohydrate, 3 Fat **Carbohydrate Choices:** 4

Tip To make a fairy princess hat, cut a 3½-inch round out of pink construction paper. Roll the paper in a cone shape so that the top comes to a point; secure it with tape, and trim the bottom so it's flat. Embellish the hat with a ribbon and yellow star candy. To make a magic wand, attach a yellow candy star and ribbons to a toothpick. Attach the wand to one hand with a small piece of tape, if necessary.

Castle Cake

Prep Time: 55 Minutes • **Start to Finish:** 4 Hours 30 Minutes • Makes 30 servings

Cake

- 2 boxes Betty Crocker SuperMoist chocolate fudge cake mix
- 2 cups water
- 1 cup vegetable oil
- 6 eggs
- Tray or cardboard (18 x 18 inches), covered with wrapping paper and plastic food wrap or foil

Frosting and Decorations

- 2 containers (1 lb each) Betty Crocker Rich & Creamy milk chocolate frosting
- 1 fudge-dipped ice cream cone
- 4 regular-size ice cream cones with pointed ends
- 5 miniature ice cream cones with pointed ends
- 1 tube (4.25 oz) white decorating icing
- Blue colored sugar
- Star-shaped candy sprinkles
- 5 rectangular vanilla sugar wafer cookies
- Pretzel sticks
- 4 red cinnamon candies
- Red string licorice
- 4 miniature peanut butter cup candies
- 4 red jujube candies
- 4 white gum balls
- 12 miniature chocolate-covered caramels

Travel to the land of castles, princes and princesses with a delicious and fun cake.

1 Heat oven to 350°F (325°F for dark or nonstick pans). Spray bottom and sides of 4 (8-inch) square pans with baking spray with flour. In large bowl, beat 1 cake mix, 1 cup of the water, ½ cup of the oil and 3 eggs with electric mixer on low speed 30 seconds, then on medium speed 2 minutes, scraping bowl occasionally. Divide batter between 2 of the pans.

2 Bake 27 to 34 minutes or until toothpick inserted in center comes out clean. Cool 10 minutes; remove from pans to cooling racks. Cool completely, about 30 minutes. Repeat with remaining cake mix, water, oil and eggs. Freeze cakes 45 minutes before cutting to reduce crumbs.

3 Trim off rounded top from each cake to make flat surfaces. On tray, place cake A (see diagram); spread with ⅓ cup of the frosting. Top with cake B; spread with ⅓ cup of the frosting. Top with cake C; spread with ⅓ cup of the frosting.

4 Cut fourth cake into quarters. Stack 2 quarter pieces on top of stacked cakes (pieces 1 and 2; see diagram), spreading 1 tablespoon frosting between them. Spread top with 1 tablespoon frosting. Cut third quarter into 2-inch square; place on center of cake stack (piece 3; see diagram). (Discard remaining cake, or reserve for another use.)

5 Reserve 2 tablespoons frosting in resealable food-storage plastic bag. To seal crumbs, spread thin layer of frosting over layered cake. Refrigerate or freeze cake 30 to 60 minutes to set frosting. Spread remaining frosting over entire cake. Place fudge-dipped cone upside down on top of cake. Place 4 regular ice cream cones upside down on corners of cake.

6 Place white decorating icing in small bowl. Dip edges of miniature cones into icing; sprinkle with blue sugar. Place upside down on top of larger cones. Top each cone with candy star, attaching with small amount of white icing.

7 Cut 1 wafer cookie in half crosswise. Cut small tip off 1 corner of bag of frosting. Pipe frosting on 2 whole cookies and 1 half cookie for window panes. Place windows on castle. Insert ends of pretzels slightly into cake for drawbridge. Place 2 cookies on drawbridge for door; press tops slightly against cake. Add cinnamon candies to doors and front of cake. Add licorice for bridge wire.

8 Place peanut butter cup candies upside down on 4 corners near top of castle. To make turrets, add red jujube candies and gum balls to peanut butter candies with small amount of white icing. Add caramels to front of cake for parapets. Store loosely covered.

1 Serving (Cake and Frosting Only): Calories 300; Total Fat 14g (Saturated Fat 3.5g, Trans Fat 2g); Cholesterol 40mg; Sodium 340mg; Total Carbohydrate 42g (Dietary Fiber 0g); Protein 2g **Exchanges:** ½ Starch, 2½ Other Carbohydrate, 2½ Fat **Carbohydrate Choices:** 3

Tip Instead of using milk chocolate frosting, create a pink castle by using either Betty Crocker Whipped strawberry or Rich & Creamy cherry frosting. This cake is perfect for a princess-themed party. Look for inexpensive tiaras and wands at your local party-supply store.

Cutting and Assembling Castle Cake

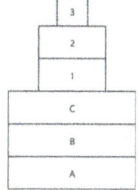

Arrange pieces on tray to form castle.

Theme Parties · 35

Metric Conversion Guide

Volume

U.S. Units	Canadian Metric	Australian Metric
¼ teaspoon	1 mL	1 ml
½ teaspoon	2 mL	2 ml
1 teaspoon	5 mL	5 ml
1 tablespoon	15 mL	20 ml
¼ cup	50 mL	60 ml
⅓ cup	75 mL	80 ml
½ cup	125 mL	125 ml
⅔ cup	150 mL	170 ml
¾ cup	175 mL	190 ml
1 cup	250 mL	250 ml
1 quart	1 liter	1 liter
1½ quarts	1.5 liters	1.5 liters
2 quarts	2 liters	2 liters
2½ quarts	2.5 liters	2.5 liters
3 quarts	3 liters	3 liters
4 quarts	4 liters	4 liters

Weight

U.S. Units	Canadian Metric	Australian Metric
1 ounce	30 grams	30 grams
2 ounces	55 grams	60 grams
3 ounces	85 grams	90 grams
4 ounces (¼ pound)	115 grams	125 grams
8 ounces (½ pound)	225 grams	225 grams
16 ounces (1 pound)	455 grams	500 grams
1 pound	455 grams	0.5 kilogram

Note: The recipes in this cookbook have not been developed or tested using metric measures. When converting recipes to metric, some variations in quality may be noted.

Measurements

Inches	Centimeters
1	2.5
2	5.0
3	7.5
4	10.0
5	12.5
6	15.0
7	17.5
8	20.5
9	23.0
10	25.5
11	28.0
12	30.5
13	33.0

Temperatures

Fahrenheit	Celsius
32°	0°
212°	100°
250°	120°
275°	140°
300°	150°
325°	160°
350°	180°
375°	190°
400°	200°
425°	220°
450°	230°
475°	240°
500°	260°

Recipe Testing and Calculating Nutrition Information

Recipe Testing:

- Large eggs and 2% milk were used unless otherwise indicated.
- Fat-free, low-fat, low-sodium or lite products were not used unless indicated.
- No nonstick cookware and bakeware were used unless otherwise indicated. No dark-colored, black or insulated bakeware was used.
- When a pan is specified, a metal pan was used; a baking dish or pie plate means ovenproof glass was used.
- An electric hand mixer was used for mixing only when mixer speeds are specified.

Calculating Nutrition:

- The first ingredient was used wherever a choice is given, such as ⅓ cup sour cream or plain yogurt.
- The first amount was used wherever a range is given, such as 3- to 3½-pound whole chicken.
- The first serving number was used wherever a range is given, such as 4 to 6 servings.
- "If desired" ingredients were not included.
- Only the amount of a marinade or frying oil that is absorbed was included.

America's most trusted cookbook is better than ever!

- 1,100 all-new photos, including hundreds of step-by-step images
- More than 1,500 recipes, with hundreds of inspiring variations and creative "mini" recipes for easy cooking ideas
- Brand-new features
- Gorgeous new design

Get the best edition of the *Betty Crocker Cookbook* today!

www.ingramcontent.com/pod-product-compliance
Lightning Source LLC
Chambersburg PA
CBHW071417290426
44108CB00014B/1860